Born From Above

by

W.B. Godbey

First Fruits Press
Wilmore,
Kentucky
c2018

Born From Above.
By W.B. Godbey.
First Fruits Press, © 2018

ISBN: 9781621718307 (print). 9781621718314 (digital), 9781621718321
(kindle)

Digital version at https://place.asburyseminary.edu/godbey/21/

For all other uses, contact:

First Fruits Press
B.L. Fisher Library
Asbury Theological Seminary
204 N. Lexington Ave.
Wilmore, KY 40390
http://place.asburyseminary.edu/firstfruits

Godbey, W. B. (William Baxter), 1833-1920.
    Born from above / by W.B. Godbey. – Wilmore, KY : First Fruits Press,
    ©2018.

    pages 35 ; cm.

    Reprint. Previously published: Greensboro, N.C. : Apostolic Messenger
    Office, [190-?]
    ISBN: 9781621718307 (print)
    1. Regeneration (Theology)   I. Title.

BT790.G622 2018

Cover design by Jon Ramsay

asburyseminary.edu
800.2ASBURY
204 North Lexington Avenue
Wilmore, Kentucky 40390

First Fruits
THE ACADEMIC OPEN PRESS OF ASBURY SEMINARY

First Fruits Press
The Academic Open Press of Asbury Theological Seminary
204 N. Lexington Ave., Wilmore, KY 40390
859-858-2236
first.fruits@asburyseminary.edu
asbury.to/firstfruits

Born from Above

By

W. B. Godbey

AUTHOR OF
"New Testament Commentaries. " "New Testament
Translation," and a great number of
other books and booklets.

PUBLISHED BY

THE APOSTOLIC MESSENGER OFFICE

GREENSBORO, N. C.

Born From Above

You see from our Lord's plain phraseology, the pure spirituality of His supernatural birth which He positively and repeatedly certifies we must have, John 3:7 "marvel not that I said unto you, ye must be born from above, "not again" as E. V. the Greek word **palm** again is not in this passage at all and a great pity, the translators ever put it in, as it flatly contradicts the teaching of Jesus, who throughout His ministry repeatedly held up the little children certifying that they were paragon members of His kingdom and that all adults, must repent, get rid of their sins, and become like little children, innocent, before they could ever enter the kingdom of heaven. If Jesus had said "again" in this passage He would have consigned to hell every child who ever died antecedently to the physical birth as "again" means a repetition and consigns to hell everybody that does not get it. Consequently if you will analyze the matter as you would see there is no chance for the mutiplied millions who have died before the physical birth. When you hear the preachers and the singers roaring out "born again" that our Savior never said it, but He did say that you must be born from above, or you cannot see the kingdom of God.

CHAPTER I

THE TRUE SPIRITUALITY OF THIS BIRTH

Satan does his best to hide the truth of God with his black wing so the people will miss it all together. and he will get them in the end. The first 20 years of my life, I saw them taking poor sinners into the church, taking them down to the creek and dipping them into the water to save their souls; thus deceiving them and running them into idolatry; the preacher taking the place of the Savior and putting the water in place of the Holy Spirit, leaving no alternative to the poor deluded soul, but like Dives Luke 16 ch. to die looking for heaven and find himself in hell. Such is the deplorable malad ministration of the false prophets, to whom the people are looking for the blessed truth of God to save their never dying souls. Jesus tells us the very opposite, that we do not go down to the creek to get this birth, but it must come down from God out of heaven, otherwise the soul is deceived and forever lost. The word Jesus used is **anoothen,** from **ana,** above and **then** the adverbial termination, and simply means from above, i.e. it does not come from a mill pond, a preacher or anything else in this world; but comes down from God out of heaven.

(a)   Born of water and spirit is the grand Gibraltar of the Campbellite heresy; repudiating the Holy Ghost and telling us, the Word is the Spirit and that you have to be immersed in order to be born of the water, as you cannot be born of a thing less than yourself; thus utterly deluding the people, so they take the preacher instead of the Savior, water in lieu of the Holy Ghost, thus fatally superinducing the inevitable result of hell instead of heaven, like Dives Luke 16 ch. who stood at the front of his church, died confidently as a Roman Catholic, looking for heaven; but so awfully disappointed to find hell. Oh how history repeats itself over and over, the people dying, receiving a grand funeral, while at the very time they are preaching them to heaven they are in hell, like Dives crying for mercy; but in vain, too late.

(b) You see Nicodemus took the Campbellite, Catholic and Mormon view, and thought our Savior meant his body; responding to Him, "how can a man be born when he is old? can he enter the second time unto his mother's womb and be born? Jesus not only corrected him but castigated him for his ignorance, as a teacher in Israel he should have known better. How strange the great Catholic world still have their feet in Nicodemus hobble and the vast majority of the Protestant world with them, taking your body to the river and putting it in water, where as here is no more allusion to your body than that of your horse, cow or dog, and Jesus so lucidly corrected the serious mistake of Nicodemus, telling him positively that he did not need anything done to his body; v 6, "That which is generated of depravity is depravity; that which is generated of spirit is spirit; thus showing clearly that the body has nothing to do at all with it; whereas every human being through fallen Adam our federal head, is generated in depravity, i.e. devil nature, which is certain to lead us into sin and down to hell; if not regenerated in Christ. The word translated flesh in this verse, is not **sooma**, which means the body; but **sarx**, which means depravity, in which every human being is generated in fallen Adam, who had lost his spiritual life by the fall, and would not transmit what he did not have. Therefore every human being is generated in Adam, totally depraved, i.e. deprived of spiritual life, and full of the satanic death, so as the old prophet that "the children go away as soon as they are born speaking lies, prone to do evil as the sparks are to go upward.

(c) Consequently if God had not "so loved the world, that He gave His only begotten Son, that whosoever believeth in Him, should not perish but have eternal life," this world would never have been anything but an hell feeder, i.e. a hog pen to fatten souls for the barbecues of the pandemonium. The innate depravity is revealed unmistakeably, Psalm 51: 5 "I was shapen in iniquity and in sin did my mother conceive me." As we have been singing since the days of Charles Wesley, Lord I am vile, conceived in sin; born unholy and unclean; sprung from the man whose guilty fall, corrupts his race and ruins all. Here and in a thousand more scriptures, we see total depravity transmitted by every human being by the fall; not meaning that we are as bad as we can be, which is not true even of the devil, as he, like all other finite beings is progressive; worse now than yesterday and getting worse all the time, as all the wicked progress inturpitude and alienation from God and proclivity to do evil; just as all the righteous, human as well as angelic, progress in holiness and divine similitude and efficiency, in the glorification of God, through the flight of eternal ages.

(d) The wonderful and glorious and redemptive scheme actually reaches every human being, the very moment the soul and body united constitute personality, which is far back in the prenatal state, five or six months antecedently to the physical birth Heb. 2:9, by the grace of Christ tasted death for every one, not every man" as E. V.; but the beautiful Greep **huper pantos**, for every one, which takes in every human being ever generated of Adäm's race, the very moment the transmission out of the fatal in the personal state supervenes, developing the consolitory fact, that the Omnipotent grace of God in Christ, actually reaches every soul, antecedently to the physical birth; so every one is

born in the kingdom of God, as you see beautifully
illustrated in the Prodigal son and his elder brother,
both of whom were born in the Father's house, i.e.
the kingdom of God, and while the younger impor-
tunately strayed away, the elder had the good fortune to get converted before he reached the re-
sponsibility, like the phophet Samuel, John the Baptist, the apostle Timothy, your humble servant and
many little ones I have seen converted in my ministry, felicitiously, antecedently to the forfeiture of
their infantile justification, which is really God's
time for every human being to be turned round as
I was through the instrumentality of my sainted
mother and introduced to my Savior, so with great
delight, I heard His voice, took Him by the hand and
started heavenward; still needing the second work
of grace to take the depravity out of me, which I
had inherited through Satan through fallen Adam
and would have at once led me into sundry wick-
edness, if God had not in His condescending mercy,
used my angel mother and my preaching father
to turn me round; as, though born in His kingdom,
that depravity turned my face away from God, if
let alone, I would have gone like the Prodigal son;
unhesitatingly away into sin; moving on from bad
to worse, till I reached the hog pen, or perhaps hell
the next station and plunged in.

(e)   Therefore I can never praise the Lord enough
for the parental influence, which blessed me with
that infantile conversion, which headed off the devil,
and permitted me to give the Lord, the innocency of
my childhood, the buoyancy of my boyhood, the
vigor of my youth, the enterprise of my young man-
hood, the aggressive campaigns, crowning life's me-
ridian, and now my declining years; preaching night
and day, economising every moment, to finish the
work He has given me to do; permitting me to preach
these sixty-two years, travel a hundred and fifty

thousand miles; four times round the historic world, and booked to go again April 1st 1918 (go with me for $500.00 as otherwise you would pay a thousand) and writing 178 books all telling the people the sure Bible way to heaven; expounding lucidly all the vital truths and exposing all the fatal current heresies, which are sweeping the whole country like withering cyclones; cutting down the Lord's pilgrims on all sides; humbugging millions of sinners with vain, silly and foolish satanic caprices; cheating them out of their souls and plunging into hell, led astray by Satan's false prophets, who did in the former dispensation superabound on all sides; "prophesying smooth things" and giving the people an easy way to heaven with which they are delighted, as they can travel along full of sin, yet like Dives destined to find themselves in hell when the journey winds up, instead of heaven, from the simple fact they neither receive the supernatural birth nor entire sanctification, which God has decreed for every soul that shall ever pass the heavenly portals and behold His glory.

(f) The Macedonian cry is rising from millions, throughout the whole world, come "over and help us," as people can only preach conterminally with their experiences; thus leaving the illimitable range for false prophets to delude the hungry multitudes as man has been denominated by philosophers, the religious animal and all the people in the world want to be saved; whereas only those who have the experience of personal salvation are competent to reveal it to others. Whereas Jesus v 6. certifies the pure spirituality of this grand **sine qua non** birth which all must receive or be forever lost; no physical aspect of it whatever, which is further confirmed v 7 in His positive proclamation "ye must be born from above," showing positively that the wonderful transaction comes down from God out of heaven.

Whereas a false interpretation of v 5, has run millions into idolatry, worshipping the water god, as
gross and superstitious as the idolatry of wood and
stone, gold silver, brass or anything else; the wrong
translation in v. 8. "the wind bloweth were it listeth.........has seriously marred our Lord's beautiful explanation of this miraculous spiritual transaction.   Why they ever put it down wind I can not
imagine, as it is not a definition of **pneuma** the word
our Savior here used which means nothing but
spirit.   That same word **pneuma** also winds up the
sentence.   Therefore if you translate it wind at the
beginning, consistency would require you so to ren-
der it at the conclusion, and it would read "the wind
bloweth were it listeth thou hearest the sound
therefore, but cans't not tell whence it cometh nor
whither it goeth; ever so is every one who is born
of the wind."   You see its utter unintelligibility.
Now let us take it just the way Jesus gave it, "The
spirit breathes on whom he will, thou hearest his
voice, but cans't not tell whence he cometh, or
whither he goest; even so is every one who is born
of the spirit."   Every sinner is is a spiritual corpse,
having ears, but hearing nothing, till the Holy
Spirit breathes on him quickening him into life,
when he hears his voice, but cannot tell his loco-
motions, just as is everyone who is born from above.
You do not understand the mysterious workings of
the Holy Spirit; yet you have the testimony of the
blind man John 9 ch. "whereas I was once blind I
now see."

(g) Here you see Jesus utterly smashes and oblit-
erates the materialistic news of Nicodemus, who
thought his body had to be born.   I know that you
can understand clearly the mistake of all the people
who apply this to water baptism which does not
reach the human soul but simply appertains to the
mortal body to which our Savior had **no reference**

whatever and not only corrected the mistake of Nicodemus but castigated him for making it because a teacher in Israel should have known better. Therefore you see there is not a drop of material water in this chapter. Learn this truth once for all as you can not afford to abide in the superstitions of the dark ages, as the promise is only to those who walk in the light.

(h) Our Savior's next sermon is to the Samaritan woman at Jacob's well, John ch. 4, N. B. The divisions into chapters and verses has no authority in it whatever and never did have; because it was never made by the inspired writers but the London printers in 1551 who have thus revealed their own ignorance of the multiplied millions reading the Bible in all coming ages. (I have seen the room in Paris, France, in which Voltaire the great infidel wrote his refutations of the Bible, in which he prophecied that in a hundred years there would not be one in the world. His statue is still standing there on the street for everybody to look at. When the hundred years, rolled away the very room in which he wrote the prophecy, certifying that by that time there would not be one in the world; was a Bible depository, crowded full of Bibles; thus showing up the falsity of the prophecy; God Himself so managing it, that the house changed hands; becoming the property of Bible publishers, who filled the old office of Satan's infidel prophet, chucked full of Bibles.)

(i) Therefore in reading your Bible you should pay no attention by chapters and verses because they were not made by the inspired writers and they really impede your efforts to study it, as those ignorant printers; frequently break the subject in two in the middle. Therefore wink at the 4 ch. division and you are at once listening to his sermon to the woman at the well in which he mentions the water seven times; whereas to Nicodemus only once; she naturally concluding that he meant the water in the well for which she walked 2 miles, as the quality and at that time of year, scarce in that country. Now see how Jesus correctes her when she said "The well is deep and you have no way to draw it up. So how will you give to me." When he informs her twice over that it does not mean the water in the well; but living water, i.e. the water of life, which is Himself and though this woman as you see from her own confession was an awful sinner, down at the bottom of slumdum; yet she got the water not out of the well for the water of life which Jesus gave her rendered her utterly oblivious to her errand, so that forgetting her pitcher she ran back to the city shouting vociferously and stirring everybody by her thrilling testimony, actually becoming the sensation of the city; her street preaching raising them all on tip toe till they clamor for her to tell them where and how she got the wonderful change; metamorphosed out of a vile sinner into a flaming gospel preacher; when she challenged them to go with her and she would actually show them the Savior of the world who had wrought the mighty work in her poor lost soul; such as I have often witnessed, such people get converted and shout till they would congregate the whole town around them, filled with curiosity to know what was the matter.

(j) A young Kentuckean in slavery time was unfortunate to have a rich father who did not put him to work and gave him plenty of money. Consequently he became a drunkard in his teens and a murderer before he reached majority and sent to the penitentiary for homicide, as he did it in a drunken row; both drunk, so they did not consider it murder in the first degree which would have hung him. He was naturally very intellectual. During

his penitentiary biennium he repented and resolved
if he ever got out he would seek the Lord till he
found Him. True to his vow he hastened at once
from the prirson to a glorious revival in which B. A.
Condiff, a mighty man of God now in glory was
preaching in Robards, Henderson Co. While seeking with all his heart, he reached the living water in
the dead hours of the night in his room; ran out
shouted all over town so vociferously, running into
houses, and hugging the people, pulling the preacher out of his bed and making him shout with him,
so by sun rise he had the entire village of 500 listening spell-bound to his thrilling testimony on the
street; pressing on to a glorious pentecostal sanctification he became a flaming gospel preacher, and
heroically led the embattled host till the Great Cap-
tain favored him with the golden harp in the succession of the silver trumpet.

(k) You see in case of this woman that she actually found the Savior who was the 'Living Water."
Reader if you have not found this Water of Life,
do not hesitate as you are still in the valley of dry
bones, without Him. Eph. 2:1, "You hath he quickened who were dead in trespasses and in sins. Here
the word for quicken is the strong Greek compound,
zooeepoyese, from **zooee,** life and **poieeo,** to create
and consequently means to create the divine life
in you. Every sinner is a spiritual corpse denominated "dead" from Alpha to Omega; positive proof
of total depravity. as total means entirely and depravity means that you are deprived of some-
thing is the divine life. Therefore total depravity
simply means that the soul of the sinner is totally
dead, which no one can dispute, because God says it.
I have been reported dead in the papers four different times, but still it is a mistake; but when God
calls me out of this body, that report will be correct. Hence the people who deny total depravity,

are to be pitied for their ignorance of God's Word and their own foolish conclusions, appertaining to Bible theology.

(1) All these scriptures show up the pure spirituality of the supernatural birth, not a drop of material water in a million miles. Isa. 55:1, "Ho every one thirsteth, come ye to the waters." In that very chapter is all the prophecy of Christ, the Jehovah of the Old Testament and the Jesus of the New, in all ages Omnipotent to save; Himself the living water, which all must have or forever perish. Therefore Eph. 2:1, "You hath He quickened," literally signifying He hath created life in you, i.e. the divine life, which is the Christ nature and life, in contradistinction to the depravity, hereditary in every human heart which is simply devil-nature, i.e. spiritual death. Hence you see in this wonderful transaction, without which every soul is forever lost, the Holy Spirit creates the divine nature, in the dead human spirit which is the water of life. Consequently when you are born of water and spirit, it is simply the glorious fact that the Holy Spirit creates the divine life in your spirit, and that life is the water, and the Holy Ghost the spirit. Consequently you are born of water and spirit, and no allusion to material water whatever.

CHAPTER II

MATERIALISTIC INFIDELITY

All religion is spirituality, as man without the spirit is simply an animal. When God created man, He had only the body and the animal soul, with His extraordinary intellect, contradistinguishing him from the lower; till God breathed into him the breath of life, i.e. spiritual life, and he became a living soul, i.e. a soul having spiritual life. The Hebrew for spirit is **ruach,** the Greek **pneuma** and the

spiritus, from which we have the English word spirit. The Hebrew says He imparted the **ruach** to men, i.e. the spirit, after He had created him. Many animals in the world, i.e. gorillas, orang-outangs and apes, look so much like people, that if dressed in human costume, you would think they were men, women and children. But(whereas no people have ever been found on the earth, who did not recognize the divinity; the untutored savage in his primeval wilds, sees God in the clouds, and hears Him in the winds; whose soul found science never taught to stray, far as the solar walks, the milky way; thus verifying the philosophic maxims; man the religious animal. The heathen are as religious as any Christian you can find; worshipping their gods so devoutedly, and all I ever saw in my travels around the world, solidly believing in the supreme God who made them and everything else, and only regarding their idols as mere souveneirs. While this is true of all human beings, down to the very lowest savages and most brutal barbarians; yet it is impossible to teach an animal anything about God; even the bipeds, the highest order of animals, which stand on their feet and use their hands like men, are utterly destitute of any form of religion; or any manifestation of a supreme being, manifested in any way; though in human form, you cannot teach them to speak nor teach them anything about the God that created them; thus conforming the conclusion of the dicotomy in contradistinction to the human tricotomy consisting of the body, soul and spirit, i.e. **soomar, psychee** and **pneuma;** corroborating the fact, that God imparted the **pneuma** to man after He had created him, **sooma** and **psychee** like all the other animals; this **pneuma** which He breathed into, conferring immortality on the **psychee** and thence transmitting it to the body, in the resurrection of the dead.

(1) As the **pneuma** i.e. the spirit is the man himself, on which the Holy Spirit operates, thus making him spiritual like Himself. In view of these facts all real religion is spiritually. Paul Rom. 1 ch. shows up these facts in his revelation of man's apostasy from God, who is a pure spirit; first into mentality as it, says "that they became vain in their imagination," the Greek **dialogisniois** meaning not only imaginations but reasonings; thus dropping down from the high plane of spirituality, to the lower plane of intellectualism, where all the great Protestant churches now stand, having lost their hold on God and drifted away on intellectualism; while the 450 million Catholics have still gone on down to the lower plane of idolatry as Paul says in this chapter, worshipping the creature instead of the "Creator who is blessed forever more." This you will see superaboundingly demonstrated in all the Catholic churches, full of images, statuary and pictures. Then Paul goes on to describe the last stage of apostasy from God, ultimating in brutality, which is the deplorable status of the 900 million heathens this day, shocking to say, actually worshipping their own genital organs as you even see demonstrated in their architecture; showing up the fact of universal veneration, peculiar to humanity, in contradistinction to the lower animals; these heathens, really the apostasy of the Patriarchal church, having by Satan's manipulation, through the rolling ages, like the river which never climbs the mountain, but always descends in his run to it uttermost destination in the fathomless, shoreless ocean; Judaism and Mohammedism, simply the apostasy of the Mosaic church, while Catholicism is the apostasy of the Pentecostal church, in which all the apostles preached and sealed their faith with their

blood; with the rolling ages incessantly descending
to the lower plane, pursuant to satanic chicanery, as
he has been on the throne of the world ever since
the fall, 2 Cor. 6:6 and utilizing his wonderful wis-
dom and strategy to drag every thing down from the
high plane of spirituality from which God created it;
sinking it lower and lower till it drops into hell
which is an eternal degradation as it has no bottom; the miserable victims sinking into a more awful woe through the flight of eternal ages.

(m) O what an incentive to every unconverted
soul to escape from his dark clutches, fly for refuge;
giving back to him all sin, actual, original, hereditary, sins of ignorance, multitudinous infirmities;
thus making for the King's highway which Jesus
built with His own bleeding hands, every step from
the city of Destruction to the New Jerusalem; no
lion on it, nor ravenous beast, toll gate; perfectly
free for all, great and small, old and young, rich and
poor ,high and low, black white, yellow, red and
brown, as God is no respector of persons, and thus
run with ever accelerating velocity till we leap with
a shout through the pearly gates, receive a golden
harp which will never get out of tune and join in the
glorious heavenly anthems, symphonies with angels,
archangels,, cherubim, seraphim, to sing on through
the flight of eternal ages.

(n) As all orthodox religion is pure spirituality;
beginning with the supernatural birth, wrought in
the heart by the Holy Ghost, thus superinducing
the birth of water and spirit which comes down from
God out of heaven and has nothing to do with the
human body, nor the mind, but simply means a glorious heavenly metamorphism of the immortal human spirit; the Holy Spirit creating His own similitude the divine life in the dead soul, which will
have the dominion over the hereditary depravity,
only at the point of the bayonet as Satan gives up

nothing without a fight, and the carnal mind the Ishmael in the heart, Gal. 4 ch. transmitted from Satan through fallen Adam our federal head and as you see in these scriptures 13 years older than Isaac, who was born not by natural generation as Ishmael, but by the supernatural intervention of the Holy Ghost, when the Lord 1900 years antecedently to His birth in Bethlehem visited Abraham in his tent at Mamre accompanied by two angels, and there announced to Sarah, the conception of Isaac, which means laughter as she was so delighted to become the mother of the heir of promise after her superannuation and survival of prolificy; thus working a real miracle in the conception of Isaac. Ishmael was 13 years old when Isaac was born, and 15 when he was weaned; having renewed the entire attention of the patriarchal home as he was the only heir till Isaac was born, when all eyes were focalized on him, thus impressing Ishmael with his own depreciation and provoking his animosity against Isaac manifested in mocked and sundry portorbation till Sarah, saw that her son was in danger, his life constantly annoyed and even threatened, as Ishmael would very likely have killed him if he had not been removed.

(o) In this allegory Abraham represents the visible church, Sarah, the invisible, i.e. Bride of Christ, the holy mother of all God's children, Hagar the fallen church, i.e. Jerusalem after she had rejected her Christ, and Ishmael the carnal members of the visible church. When Sarah demanded the removal of the bond woman and her son; Abraham tenderhearted for them, hesitated till he would consult God in person, who responded to him unhesitatingly, "Sarah your wife is correct; Go ahead and cast out the bond woman and her son." Therefore he proceeds without delay and they were never in the patriarchal home any more.

(p) Consequently Isaac was sole heir to the prince-

ly fortune having everything his own way and no
one to disturb him; thus a brilliant type of Christ,
who must reign in your heart and mine without a
rival; all antagonisms having been removed, when
Ishmael, i.e. old Adam and Hagar, the fallen church
are taken away.   In this notable transaction, con-
nected with the holy family we see two definite
conspicious, prominent, divine intervention, i.e. the
supernatural birth of Isaac, and then followed by the
ejectment of the bond woman and her son; thus
showing forth conspicuously these two grand and
prominent supernaturalisms constituting the magni-
ficent globe of the new creation; in regeneration a
world created in the heart, and in sanctification a
world destroyed and taken out of the heart, the
former the supernatural birth, coming down from
God out of heaven, ushered in by the creation of
the divine life in the heart, the Christ nature in
the soul, which is the immediate work of the Holy
Ghost, thus gloriously and triumphantly superinducing the birth of water and spirit.

(q) Under the wonderful Constantinian revival,
which normally followed his conversion to Christianity, A. D. 321, when he did his uttermost to prevail
on all the people in the world as his crown radiated
the rays of an unsetting sun and his scepter swept
the circumference of the globe; thus giving him universal influence over the popular mind, which he
nobly exercised for the glory of God doing his uttermost to stop all idol worship and prevail on everybody to worship the Christian's God, the Omnipotent Creator, Preserver and Benefactor of all things
animate and inanimate, especially did he strive to
stop all idol worship in Rome, the world's capital;
but could not because Rome had fought 753 years in
the conquest of all nations of the earth; meanwhile
she recognized all their gods and had temples built
for them in the city, many of which stand to this

day, and I have been in them; among them the great
Pantheon, so beautiful a perfect circle 200 feet in
diameter and in altitude, with no windows; but a cir-
cular aperture 32 feet in diameter in the center
through which the sun shines down and the rains
fall, built by the Emperors 2100 years ago and dedi-
cated to all the gods; still in use and free for all re-
ligions, so the holiness people can now go in and
preach as much as they please.

(r) As Constantine, signally failed to stop all idol
worship in Rome he went a thousand miles toward
the rising sun to Byzantium, which had stood on the
Bosphorus connecting the Mediterranean and Euxine
seas, and separating Asia and Europe a thousand
years and never grown much. So when the Emperor
came thither and selected seven great, rich and
beautiful hills on which to build the world's new capital calling it New Rome as that city stands on seven
mountains, walking all the way round it accompanied by the enthusiastic throng marking the place
where he put down his foot as he claimed to be guid-
ed by the Unseen One; there they built the wall
which Constantine named New Rome, but never
could make it stick as the grateful multitude would
name it for him, Constantinople, a compound Greek
word which simply means city of Constantine. He
ever lent a solitary heathen temple rise in it. Under
his imperial influence Christianity received a wonderful boom in all the earth.

(s) Consequently great and venerable heathen
temples with thousands of members, walloped over
turning Christian, the priests turning preachers and
the members falling in line with astounding unani-
mity, the great and valuable edifice, becoming a
Christian church. Of course the revival enthusiasm,
inspired by imperial precept and example, swept
great nations like a tornado; many of them actually
finding the Lord and getting saved, while the rank

and file halted with church joining, baptism, and
sacrament, in the sweep of enthusiasm of course receiving impulsive blessings, in the direction of con-
versation, but not reaching the real experience.
When the good old saints who had stood the storms
of persecution, for 253 year after Nero's persecu-
tionary edict; their fathers and mothers having
been cast to the wild beasts and devoured in the Coliseum who poured their money into the imperial
treasury, for the demoniacal curiosity of seeing the
Christians eaten up by the wild beasts; even crowd-
ing that great theater which seated a hundred thousand spectators, all classes, with their seats graded
off, the royal family and the princes down close to
them, so they had a good chance to witness the
bloody tragedies; then the patricians, farther back
and higher up, as the seats were elevated, so they
could see from all parts of the Coliseum, running a
hundred and sixty feet high; the Plebeians still
farther back, and the slaves, last of all, far up at the
top.   The price of the sights graded according to
proximity and character of the seats likewise; the
slaves farthest back and highest up with no seats
and paying but a pittance admission fee.

(t) These old Christians who had passed through
the bloody years of persecution; so wonderfully sur-
prised over the wonderful conversion of the Emper-
or, almost shouted themselves to death, and in the
order or line, the years rolling on they soon passed
away to heaven; followed by a grand crop, who actually got saved during the life of the emperor, who
thus with a mighty host, shouted his way up to
heaven; succeded by Julian on the throne of the
world, cognomened in history the apostate, because
he went back to the old heathen idolatry, doing his
utmost to restore it everywhere, and of course the
normal trend was to bring it into the Christian
churches.   Therefore they made images of Christ

and all the apostles, the Virgin Mary, the Arch angel
Gabriel, Michael and others; thus filling up their
churches with images, as you now see in the great
Catholic world, both Greek and Roman; thus prac-
tically returning back to idolatry; meanwhile many
of course pressed through and found the Lord, fly-
ing up to heaven with shouts, as the generations
passed away; therefore the great Constantinian revival was blessed of the Lord with the eternal salvation of vast multitudes, washed in the blood of the
Lamb, and saved to the uttermost, now shouting
around the effulgent throne; yet as the good ones
fought the battle through, died and went to heaven,
rising generations took their place and never got
saved, and then brought the church, deeper down
into idolatry, as we now to our sorrow see the great
Catholic world, deluged with sin and flooded with
idolatry, till we can hardly tell them from the
other; the difference simply consisting in the fact,
the former have Bible names, and worship the Virgin Mary, Peter. the apostles, saints and angels,
whereas the latter have the nomeniture of Budd-
hism, Brahmanism, Grand Lama, foe, Goaraster,
Confucius, etc.; thus verifying the philosophic max-
im, that man is the religious animal, under all sir-
cumstance everywhere religious, yet none of the
multitudes having salvation, but that of Christ, Acts
6:12 "No other name given under heaven among
men, by which we can be saved," who always exe-
cutes His mighty works, giving the sinner the
supernatural birth, which comes down from God out
of heaven, and the Christian the baptism of the
Holy Ghost with fire, which destroys every thing
transmitted to us from the fall through Adam our
federal head.

(u) With the fall of Rome, A. D. 646, only a
hundred and fifty years after the conversion of Constantine, Ancient civilization passed away, as she

was its only upholder; having built great roads into
every nation under heaven, for the convenience of
all to vocalize their mercantile and social interests
in this mistress of the earth, who fought 753 years,
actually subjugating all nations, and focalizing the
interest of the whole world in that great and brilliant metropolis and capital.

(v) The wild nations clustering around the north,
Pole, the Goth, the Vandals, Huns and Heruli, the
ancestors of great Russia at the present day, living
so far north, that Roman soldiers could not endure
the severity of the winters, as Italy protected from
the north winds and blizzards by the great Alpine
Range, and so fair to the tropical sun as to enjoy a
semi-tropical climate, so very genial as to have no
winter to amount to anything; but perrenial spring,
summer and autumn. For these reasons that focalized military empire held but a loose grip on these
hardy, wild nations; hovering round the north pole.
Therefore when they followed those great academ-
ized roads in their curiosity journey to the world's
metropolis, where the golden house of the emperor
and the silver houses of five thousand senators living round him, and constituting his council board,
in the administration of the whole world, proved
too strong a temptation for those avaricious barbarians, who began their invasions toward Rome, in
the days of Paul and Peter, under the reign of
Nero, and continued them at intervals of about 30
years, i.e. each revolving generation, over a hundred
years, till they finally reached the city, took it by
storm, entered the gates, where an enemy had not
trodden in six hundred years; spent a whole week
gathering the gold and silver from the palaces,
temples and shrines, which Rome in her conquest
throughout the world 753 years had spoilated from
every nation under heaven and gathered thither,
surrounded by a wall so great and impregnable, that

they actually believe that the gods had built, and it could not be taken, but it would stand for ever; thus currently adopting the presumption, cognomen, Eternal City, verily believing it would stand for ever.

(w) It took the barbarian armies a whole week to gather the gold and silver at the expiration of which they returned home; common soldiers, having become millionaires, the army lad, too poor ti buy a breakfast, when he entered the city, having to employ a donkey to carry his purse of gold and silver, as it would have broke their own back. As these barbarians had conquered the world, and owned it all and had no learning, and of course no appreciation of it, therefore the schools everywhere depleted and evansce, leaving the world wrapped in darkness, denominated in history the Dark Ages, which lasted a thousand years; meanwhile not a civil magistrate on the globe was able to force his authority; marauding bands going everywhere in the darkness of the night, taking everything they wanted, and killing the people when it was necessary to get it. Consequently in every community the people gathered around the bravest man, recognizing him as their leader and protector, (once in a railroad wreck at a rural junction, a great crowd of us had to wait all night, listening for the whistle all the time and the wires cut by robbers so we could not hear anything and crowded like sardines in a can, very few having seats, and oh the roughest men I ever knew, their talk so diabolical, it was actually alarming; a few women with us, and only one room, when I proceded to beg of them to desist, if not for the Lord's sake, for the sake of those women, as well as the Christian men among us, when the women came pressing their way through the crowd to my presence and saying, "we place ourselves in your care." I mention this little incident in my life to help you to conceive the state of things in the dark

ages, when the barbarians had the whole world in
their hands, and the light of civilization went out
in the gloom of barbaric midnight; robbers having the run in every community, so the people
rallied around, the bravest, strongest, influential
man, put themselves in his care and under his lead-
ership and protection, when he selected the highest
mountain in the community and had them all build a
great and formidable castle on its summit, surrounded by an immense impregnable wall, only entered by a solitary great iron gate, fastened with
indeferable bars, so the people could all move in
there thither and sleep secure from the robbers,
ready to cut their throats and take everything they
had, meanwhile of course they armed themselves
and fight the marauders when necessity thus developing throughout the world, what is known as
the Feudal system, as feud means Lord, is was a
system of lords and tenants, which everywhere pre-
vailed; the people only living in the villages thus
protected by the wall and going out in the day
time and doing their work, cultivating their crops,
which they gather at maturity and stored in the
walled city. We have that state of things now in
India, China, Japan and other Oriental countries,
where the darkness of paganism and bloodthirsts,
Mohammedism, shall reign.

 (x) As we travel on the cars all over the country
throughout the whole world, we will see on the mountain summits these old castles, which were built
during the dark ages and still survive, impressive
souveneirs of the centuries, fled and gone and num-
bered with the antediluvian ages. During that
memorable reign of Satan (as it was his millenium,
which he manipulated to shove in before God had
succeeded in the inauguration of His) ; meanwhile
the light of Christianity shown as a very dim taper,
so awfully mixed up with the superstitions of idol-

atry, as not one man in a thousand or one woman in twenty thousand could read or write, and the priest was looked upon as the oracle of God, and the one who could invent most ceremonies was considered the smartest. Arius lived in the second century and preached that Jesus was only a man and not God, as the Unitarians do now. Consequently an awful controversy sprang up, Arians and Trinitarians which were rife through all the dark ages.

(y) Meanwhile the latter instituted trine immersion for baptism, in order to enforce the Trinity; immerse you the first time right side downward, then lift you up and immerse you left side downward in the name of the Son, and then lift you up and dip your face foremost in the name of the Holy Ghost. The single immersion we cannot trace but a few centuries back, when in the 16th century at Providence, R. I., Roger Williams, a baptist preacher had Ezekiel Hollaman immerse him in water and then he turned around and immersed him; thus the ana baptists starting the single dip eventually dropping the syllable ana which means again and thus becoming the baptist church which is now spread over the earth in both hemispheres. I know many of them claim to have originated from John the Baptist which is utterly untrue; as we cannot trace them back but a few centuries when we run into the ana baptists which originated during the middle ages and received their cognomen for rejecting infant baptism and thus rebaptizing the people, as the name signifies. In our efforts to trace immersion back to its origin, we soon run out of the single dip, and have to take the trine immersionists -vnoareacl the time for all good men to come to the which we trace back to about the close of the 3rd century; when that controversy between the Arians and Trinitarians was under grand headway, and there can be no doubt but it was adopted in order to enforce the Trinitarians view. They even interpolated a verse in the Bible, 1st John 5:8, "Father, Son, and Spirit" the three that have witness in heaven, which is not in the original at all. We have the three that bear witness in the earth, the Spirit, the water, and the blood; but not a word of that verse which gives the three heavenly witnesses. Thus the Trinitarians interpolated that verse in the Bible and invented the trine immersion in order to give them the victory over the Rrians who were pressing them so hard; thus making a great mistake, as they were right all the time and did not need any more than they already had to make thteir cause as strong as it can be. At present 49 out of every 50 of the Christian world are trinitarians; thus the unitarian cause having but one against 49. Recently it was somewhat revived in America by the election of Pres. Taft. When they reported it on him, I though it was political rivalry and wrote him a personal letter which he answered candidly in the affirmative stating that he was a member of that church.

(z) As immersion is not in the Bible, old nor new, nor anything in it which has that meaning ever used for baptism. **Catapontidzoo** Matt. 18:6 and **Buthizoo** 1 Tim. 5:9, both mean immersion; but neither ever used a single time for baptism. As immerse is a pure Latin word while baptize is a Greek word; if the apostles and John the Baptist had used it, it would certainly abound in the Latin Bible which was translated during the Apostolic Age, having not only Apostolical diagnosis but in document. The very fact that it is not in the Latin Bible which this moment lies before my eyes and I have this session carried a class through the whole New Testament and certify you that the word is not in it a single time, nor any other word which ever means immerse. That they thought the Apostolic practice was immersion and put in those statements when there is nothing of it in the original. Phillip and the Eunuch, Acts 8 ch. is regarded as the strongest. I have been there eight times, where it took place, now called Phillip's fountain because there he baptized the Eunuch. It is on the back bone of the mountain range running all the way through Pensular Palestine; the Great sea only 40 miles west and Dead Sea 30 miles east, not room for a river and none nearer than the Jordan 70 miles, and is simply a water spout the size of my finger shoot out of the rock on the left hand side of the road as we go south; limpid, clear and bright, much appreciated as water is so scarce in that region; they catch it all, coming a long way for it; every time I saw it, recognizing it by a group of women standing round it, each one with her water pot, an earthen vessel, jug shape, different sizes, ready at her time to put the mouth under the spout and hold it till it runs full, no stream running away, as they catch it all for use; a stone trough, under it to catch any that may fall when no vessel is held under it, that animals may have it.

(z) On my first tour, I was entirely alone, the second time accompanied by two young men, who leaped from the carriage the moment it stopped opposite the fountain, my old guide who was born in Jerusalem and still lives there having spent his whole life escorting travelers, certifying, with Bedaker guide book, used by all travelers in that country that this is the identical place where Philip baptized the Eunuch. As the earth is so hard and rocky little water falling in the exchange vessels stands there in a puddle, the women barefoot standing in it, and I saw those two young men, "both go down into the water and both come up out of it (just that puddle.) When they got into the carriage I ask them if they got their feet wet, and they said "no." They just had on shoes. Hence

you see the foolishness of taking that statement,
going in and coming out for immersion, when it does
not mean it in practical life, in one case in a million.

(a) Matt. 17 ch. we see the collector call on Jesus
and Peter in Capernum to pay their temple assess-
ment the aidrachma, a coin of thirty cents assessed
on every Jew for the support of the temple. When
Jesus sent Peter to the sea to catch the fish and get
the stater (a coin of sixty cents out of its mouth,
come and pay these assessments; do you believe that
Peter waded into the sea waist deep to catch that
fish with hook and line? You know he did not as
no body but an idiot would have waded in, when he
could catch it just as well standing on the bank.
Why do I give you that case? Because it is the
strongest in the Bible used by immersionists and you
see there is nothing in it for them. Peter had heard
the Eunuch read Isa. 2:15 "so will He (Christ)
sprinkle many nations." He was reading from the
Greek septuagint which has no division into chap-
tres, hence you see sprinkling the only baptism you
can find in the Bible was in Philip's text and no
chance for anything else, as no immersion water
there anywhere about. Every other case is just as
easily explained as this. Good Lord keep us from
following any thing but thy precious and infallible
Word.

(b) These prepositions, which are no argument at
all and the strongest passage in the Greek, Mark
1: 8, Luke 3:16, Acts 1:5, Acts 11:16 and Heb. 10:
22 in which we have the testimony of John the Baptist, Jesus, Peter, Mark, Paul, Luke and Apostles
all certifying that they handled the water and not
the people; as in these five passages, we have the
Greek, without any preposition, **hudati**, water used
in the dative of instrumentality, certifying that
they handled it and not the people. All the statuary

corroborates this conclusion, representing Jesus standing and John pouring the water on his head. Paul standing and Ananias pouring the water on his head; not a trace of immersion in the Bible, can you find to save your life.

(c) What about the burial? It is like all the balance, you cannot find the human body buried in water by baptism to save your life. It is the old man, Rom. 6 ch. and Col. 2 ch. which is not your body at all but as it says "the body of sin" after it has been crucified by the baptism of the Holy Ghost which Jesus gives as it says in that same scripture; called old because it is the devil nature in you and as old as the devil, and after crucifixion this old dead body buried into the death of Christ as that very scripture says and left here forever "if you let the devil raise him up the last state is worse than the first and hell is your doom." Hence the application of this to the human body is down right falsehood and hell hatched humbuggery to deceive you and keep you from giving to Jesus and seeking His baptism, with the Holy Ghost and fire, which alone can crucify the sin personality in your heart, and thus keep you out of hell. As every sin personality which is not crucified and buried in the atonement will be buried into hell, proving the devil's millstone round your neck, dragging you down whither you'll sink forever, as hell has no bottom. Good Lord deliver you from Satan's false prophets, preaching his lies all over the country and deceiving the people, till they go to the preacher instead of Jesus and the water instead of the Holy Ghost and wind up like Dives Luke 16 "in hell instead of heaven."

CHAPTER III

ANTAGONISM TO SANCTIFICATION

Do you know that all the fight against "sancti-fication without which no one shall see the Lord" Heb. 12: 14, is by people who have never been "born from above' or have backslidden. This conclusion you may depend on as sanctification is gloriously homogenious with regeneration, simply more on the same line; the former giving you a new heart and the latter a clean heart; as the Holy Ghost must give you this new heart in your old fallen soul, which is full of hereditary depravity, which will rise in all sorts of evil tempers, passion, lust and predilection, and with the help of the devil defend you in spiritual combat and drag you down, so you will die a good church member but find yourself in a backslider's hell, if you do not, go on to perfection (true reading be carried into perfection, as Jesus is standing by with his omnipotent arms outstretch-ed and ready to carry you into a clean heart and perfect love if you will only give him a chance. As King James' translators did not have it they thought you had to go on a long time to get it; whereas the Holy Ghost never said go on; but **pharoomehha**, from **phero**, which does not mean to go but to carry; showing that they had no right to put down go on to perfection as the blessed Holy Spirit says let us be carried to perfection. Therefore reader tip your hat to Satan, giving him back all the imbred sin, you ever inherited, as you get it, from him and it belongs to him, fall in His arms and raise the shout of victory, as you trust Him fully to give you a clean heart and sanctify you wholly).

(d) You can only keep your regeneration, by press-ing directly on into sanctification which is God's will, 1 Thess. 4:3, and consequently you have noth-ing to do but take your blessed Heavenly Father's

will and raise the shout. I entreat you to settle this
wonderful salvation problem with God alone and
warn you against Satan's lasso tossed so adroitly
by his false prophets on all sides. If they had the
experience they would not preach as they do; but in
a succession of John the Baptist instead of having
you come to them and let them take you to the
water god, they would send you at once to the
Lamb of God that taketh away the sin of the world
John 1: 29. Reader I claim for you this glorious experience "born from above" and "sanctified wholly."
Be sure you get it and tell everybody you meet.

www.ingramcontent.com/pod-product-compliance
Lightning Source LLC
Chambersburg PA
CBHW030009040426
42337CB00012BA/708